# YOGA ANATOMY & PHYSIOLOGY

*Understanding the Body to Teach Yoga Safely and Intelligently*

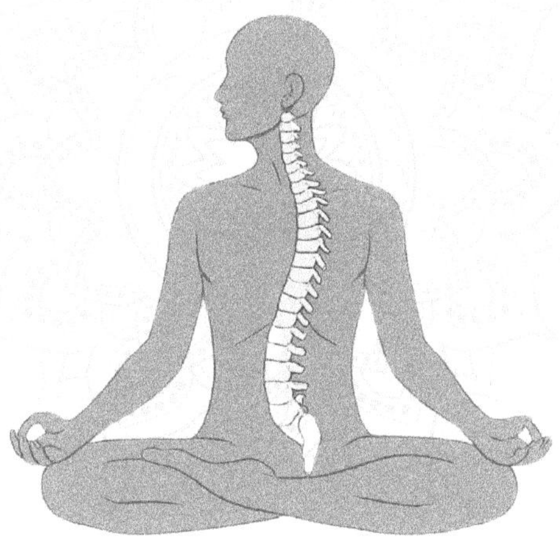

Published by:

**YOGANTA**

**Yoga Alliance Registered School**

Location: Hyderabad, India

Edition: May 2025

Website: www.yoganta.in

Email: hello@yoganta.in

YOGANTA
HEALTH | PEACE | HARMONY

**Yoga Anatomy & Physiology for Yoga Teachers**

Compiled by Raushan Yoganta

First Edition – May 2025



ISBN: **978-93-343-0758-0**

Published by Raushan Yoganta, Hyderabad, India

www.yoganta.in | hello@yoganta.in

# TABLE OF CONTENTS

# Introduction

In the world of yoga, movement is medicine—but only when guided with understanding and awareness.

This book, **Yoga Anatomy & Physiology for Yoga Teachers,** is designed to give you a practical foundation in anatomy and physiology from a yoga teacher's perspective. You don't need to memorize every muscle or become a medical expert. What you do need is the ability to observe bodies intelligently, cue safely, and respect the uniqueness of every student.

Here, we explore how bones, joints, muscles, and systems of the body all interact within the practice of yoga. You'll learn not just where the hamstrings are, but how to apply anatomical knowledge to real-life teaching—from alignment to injury prevention.

The goal isn't to impress your students with science. It's to serve them with safety, clarity, and confidence—while deepening your own connection to your body.
Welcome to the anatomy of awareness.

*Wish You Health. Peace. Harmony*

In gratitude,

**Raushan Yoganta**
*Founder & CEO, Yoganta*

# Chapter 1: Introduction to Human Anatomy

## Introduction to Human Anatomy

### Why Yoga Teachers Need Basic Anatomy?

Many yoga teachers come to the mat through experience and passion. But without a basic understanding of how the body works, it's easy to unintentionally: Overstretch joints, Overload muscles, Cause or worsen injury in students.

As a yoga teacher, your role goes beyond guiding students into poses - you guide them into their own bodies. Having a working knowledge of anatomy helps you:

- Teach safely and confidently
- Understand how each pose affects the body
- Recognize **individual differences** in flexibility and strength
- Adapt postures for various needs or limitations
- Communicate **clearly and credibly**

You don't need to memorize every bone and muscle - but knowing **how movement happens, where stress builds, and how alignment supports safety** is essential.

### What Are Anatomy, Physiology & Biomechanics?

- **Anatomy** is the study of the structure of the human body.
- **Physiology** is the study of how the body systems function.
- **Biomechanics** is how these structures move and work together during physical activity (like yoga!).

In this chapter, we explore anatomy **not as a medical subject**, but as a **practical tool** to help you move, teach, and heal with more awareness.

## Yoga Anatomy vs. Medical Anatomy

| Focus | Medical Anatomy | Yoga Anatomy |
|---|---|---|
| Purpose | Diagnosis, treatment | Self-awareness, injury prevention |
| Approach | Body as object | Body as lived experience |
| Emphasis | Pathology, intervention | Breath, movement, energy, healing |
| Application | Clinical, emergency, surgical use | Daily life, yoga, mindful movement |

## Applying Anatomy in Your Yoga Teaching

Use anatomy to:

- **Design balanced sequences** that target muscle groups
- **Spot poor alignment** and offer safe corrections
- **Understand injuries** and adapt poses appropriately
- **Educate students** without overwhelming them

You don't need to be a doctor - but you do need to know:

- How the **bones and joints** move
- Which **muscles are active** in a pose
- How **breath and nervous system** respond to yoga

# Chapter 2: Skeleton System & Joint Movements

**Skeletal System** in the human body is the framework of bones and connective tissues that provides **structure, support, and protection** to the body. It plays a crucial role in movement, blood cell production, and mineral storage. All of which are essential for yoga practice. Understanding bones, joints, and alignment helps yoga teachers guide students safely, prevent injuries, and improve posture and flexibility.

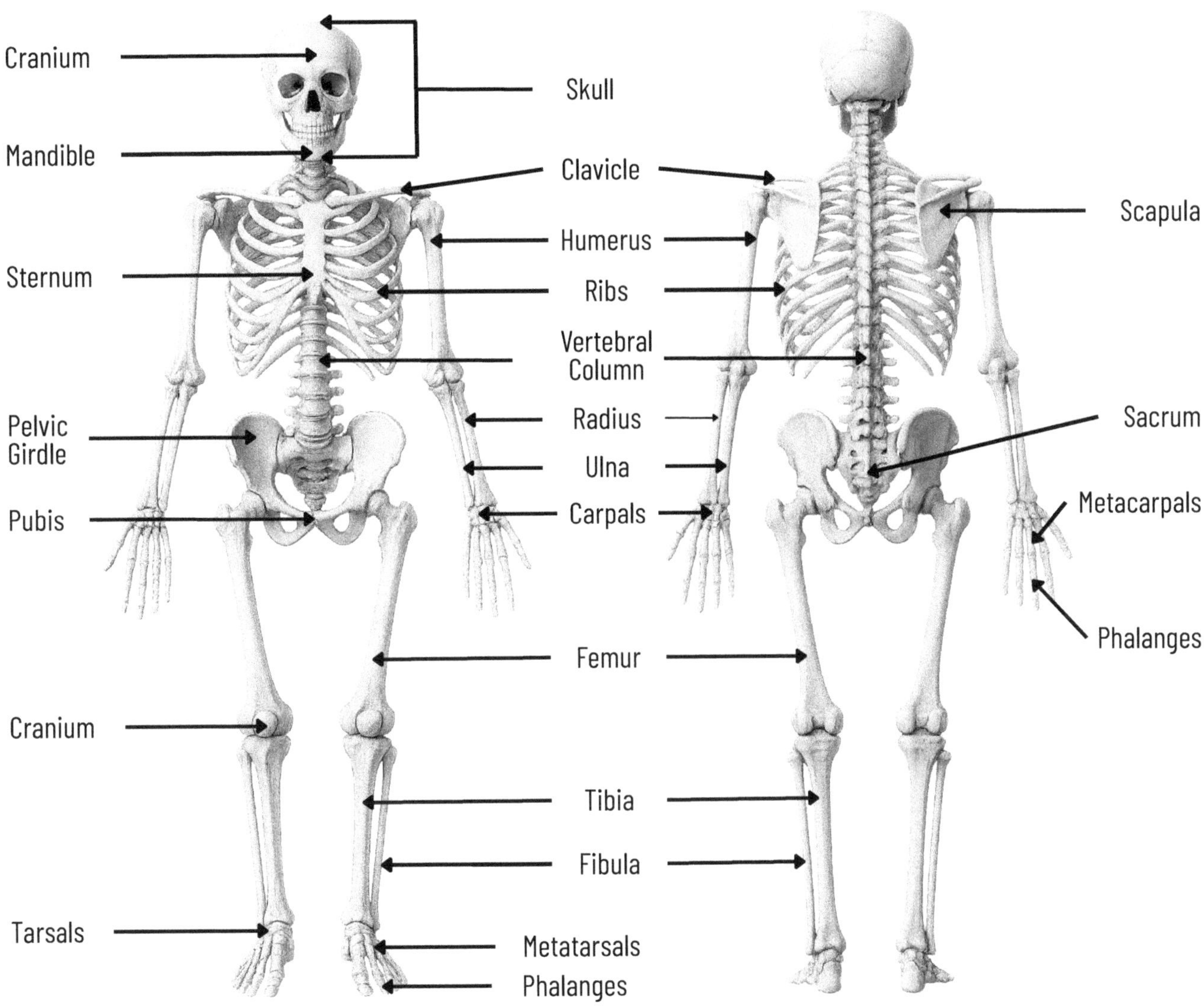


Anterior - Front View

Posterior - Back View

## Functions of the Skeletal System

- **Support** – Provides structural support for the body and maintains posture.
- **Protection** – Shields vital organs (e.g., skull protects the brain, rib cage protects the heart and lungs).
- **Movement** – Works with muscles to enable movement.
- **Blood Cell Production** – Bone marrow produces red and white blood cells.
- **Mineral Storage** – Stores calcium and phosphorus, essential for bone strength and metabolic functions.
- **Endocrine Regulation** – Bones release hormones that influence blood sugar and fat storage.

## Types of Bones in the Human Skeleton

The human body has **206 bones**, categorized into:

- **Long Bones** – Support weight and facilitate movement (e.g., femur, humerus).
- **Short Bones** – Provide stability and some movement (e.g., carpals, tarsals).
- **Flat Bones** – Protect organs and provide attachment points for muscles (e.g., skull, ribs, scapula).
- **Irregular Bones** – Have complex shapes for specific functions (e.g., vertebrae, pelvis).
- **Sesamoid Bones** – Embedded in tendons to reduce friction (e.g., patella/kneecap).

## Divisions of the Skeletal System

**1. Axial Skeleton (80 bones)** – Central framework of the body:

- **Skull** (Cranium and facial bones)
- **Spine** (Vertebral Column)
- **Rib Cage** (Ribs & Sternum)

**2. Appendicular Skeleton (126 bones)** – Bones of the limbs and movement:

- **Shoulder girdle** (clavicle, scapula)
- **Arms and hands** (humerus, radius, ulna, carpals, metacarpals, phalanges)
- **Pelvic girdle** (hip bones)
- **Legs and feet** (femur, tibia, fibula, tarsals, metatarsals, phalanges)

## Joints & Connective Tissues

- **Joints** – Allow movement (e.g., hinge joints in knees, ball-and-socket in hips).
- **Cartilage** – Cushions joints and prevents bone friction.
- **Ligaments** – Connect bones to bones, providing stability.
- **Tendons** – Attach muscles to bones, aiding movement.

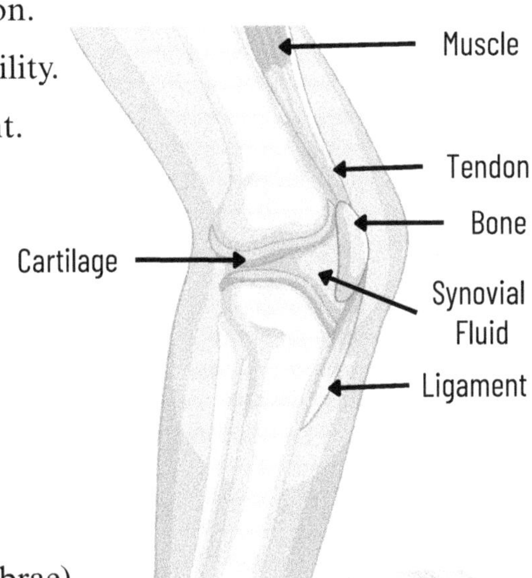


## Major Joints & Their Movements

**Joints** are where two or more bones meet. They are the **engines of mobility** in yoga practice.

### 3 Types of Joints:

1. **Fibrous** – Immovable (e.g., skull sutures)
2. **Cartilaginous** – Slightly movable (e.g., between vertebrae)
3. **Synovial** – Freely movable and most relevant in yoga

**Synovial joints** (like the shoulder, hip, knee) are surrounded by fluid-filled capsules that allow smooth motion.

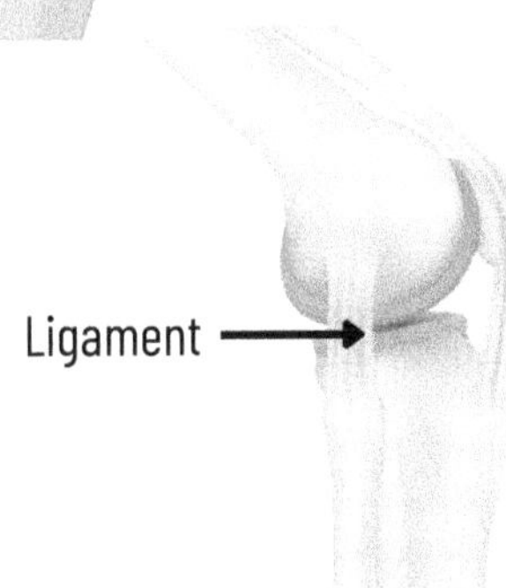


## Major Joint Movements in Yoga:

| **Movement** | **Description** | **Example Pose** |
|---|---|---|
| Flexion | Bending a joint to decrease angle | Forward fold (Uttanasana) |
| Extension | Straightening to increase angle | Backbend (Bhujangasana) |
| Abduction | Moving away from midline | Triangle pose (Trikonasana) |
| Adduction | Moving toward the midline | Eagle pose (Garudasana) arms/legs |
| Rotation | Turning around an axis | Twisting pose (Ardha Matsyendrasana) |
| Circumduction | Circular movement combining flexion, extension | Arm circles |

# Types of Synovial Joints in the Human Body

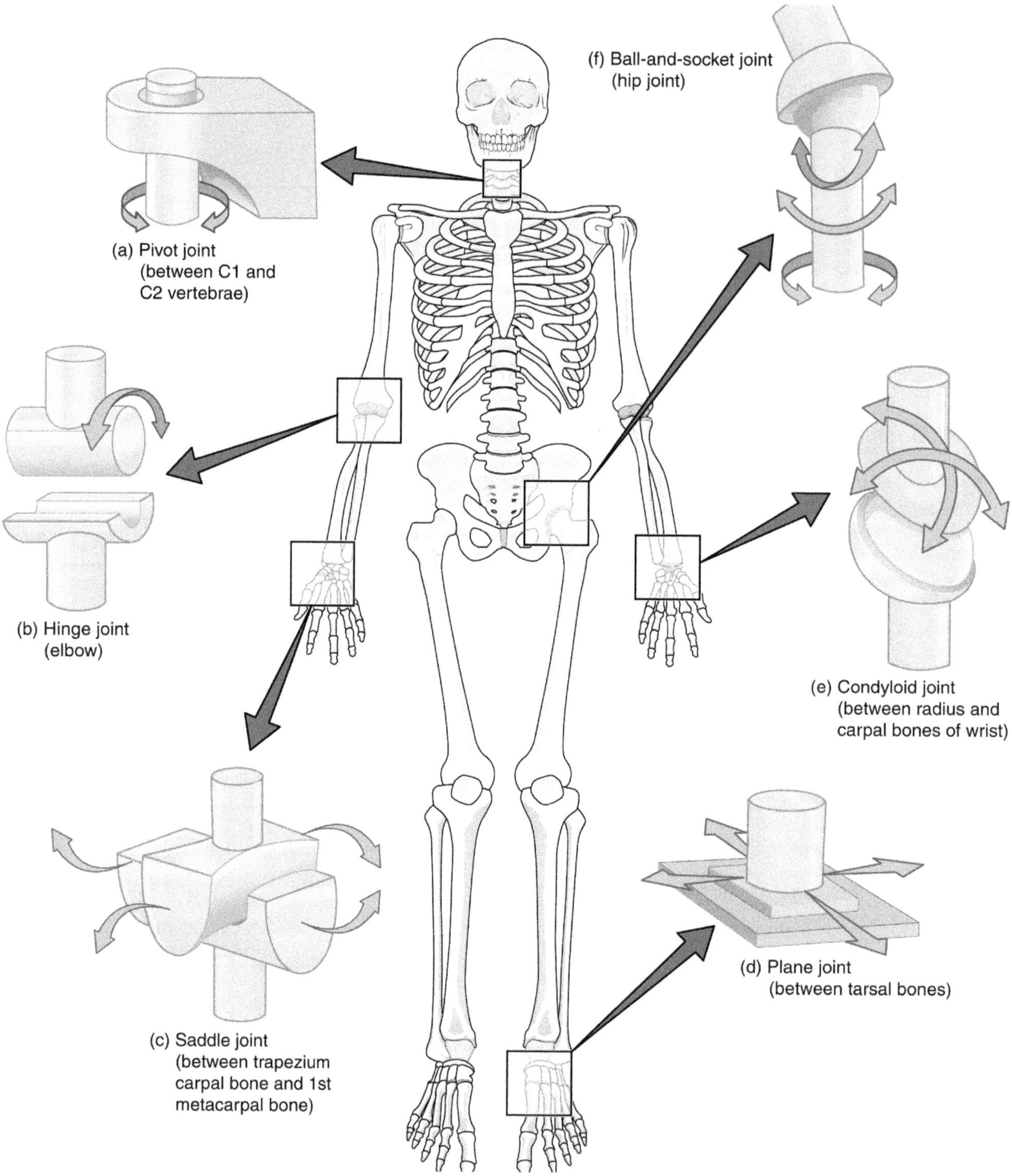


Image source: OpenStax

Access for free at https://openstax.org/books/anatomy-and-physiology/pages/1-introduction

## Major Synovial Joints in Yoga:

Understanding **synovial joints** helps yoga practitioners improve mobility, prevent injury, and refine alignment in asanas. These joints allow smooth movement by reducing friction through **synovial fluid** and **cartilage cushioning**.

### Ball-and-Socket Joints (Hips & Shoulders)

- **Movement**: Multi-directional (flexion, extension, abduction, adduction, rotation).
- **Yoga Application:**
  - **Hips**: Essential for deep hip-openers (*Lotus Pose, Warrior Poses*).
  - **Shoulders**: Allow overhead arm movements (*Downward Dog, Wheel Pose*).

### Hinge Joints (Knees, Elbows, Fingers, Toes, Ankles)

- **Movement**: Flexion & extension (bending and straightening).
- **Yoga Application**:
  - **Knees**: Key for lunges and standing postures (*Warrior Poses, Chair Pose*).
  - **Elbows**: Support weight in arm balances (*Chaturanga, Crow Pose*).
  - **Ankles**: Provide stability in balance poses (*Tree Pose, Warrior III*).

### Pivot Joints (Neck & Forearm)

- **Movement**: Rotation around a central axis.
- **Yoga Application**:
  - **Neck**: Allows head rotation in **Twisting Poses** (*Revolved Triangle, Seated Twist*).
  - **Forearm**: Enables palms to turn upward/downward (*Upward-Facing Dog, Chaturanga*).

### Gliding Joints (Wrist, Ankles, Spine Facet Joints)

- **Movement**: Small sliding or gliding motions.
- **Yoga Application:**
  - **Wrists**: Micro-movements adjust pressure in weight-bearing poses (Plank, Handstand).
  - **Ankles**: Assist in smooth transitions between standing and balancing poses (Warrior I & III).
  - **Spine (Facet Joints)**: Enable spinal flexion, extension, lateral flexion, and rotation (Cobra, Cat-Cow, Twists).

### Condyloid Joints (Wrist & Ankle - Hybrid Movement)

- **Movement**: Multi-directional (flexion, extension, slight rotation).
- **Yoga Application:**
  - **Wrist**: Allows fluid hand positioning in Mudras and Weight-bearing Poses (Downward Dog).
  - **Ankle**: Provides both flexibility & stability, critical in standing balances (Eagle Pose, Dancer's Pose).

## Understanding Range of Motion (ROM)

**Range of Motion (ROM)** refers to how far a joint can move safely and effectively in different directions. It is influenced by biomechanics, individual anatomy, and lifestyle factors.

### Factors Affecting ROM

Several elements determine a person's flexibility and joint mobility:

- **Genetics** – Bone structure, ligament elasticity, and muscle composition vary among individuals.
- **Age & Gender** – Younger individuals and women tend to have greater flexibility due to joint laxity.
- **Practice & Lifestyle** – Regular movement (yoga, sports) enhances ROM, while inactivity leads to stiffness.
- **Past Injuries & Medical Conditions** – Scar tissue, arthritis, or past trauma can restrict joint mobility.
- **Muscle Strength & Tension** – Tight muscles limit ROM, while balanced strength & flexibility allow safe movement.

## ROM in Yoga: Balancing Flexibility & Stability

In yoga, improving ROM is about finding the balance between flexibility and stability:
Functional Flexibility – Mobility that supports movement without compromising joint integrity.

**Joint Stability** – Engaging muscles around a joint to prevent hypermobility and strain.

**Active Range of Motion (AROM)** - Movement performed using muscle engagement without external assistance (gravity, props, hands, or another person).

**Passive Range of Motion (PROM)** - Movement where an external force (gravity, props, hands, or a teacher) moves the joint beyond its active control.

## Common Joint Injuries in Yoga

Understanding where joints are **vulnerable** helps prevent harm.

| Joint | Common Injury | Cause |
|---|---|---|
| Shoulders | Strain, dislocation, impingement | Improper Chaturanga or deep binds |
| Knee | Meniscus tear, ligament strain | Misaligned foot-knee-hip in lunges or twists |
| Wrist | Overuse injury | Excess weight-bearing in arm balances |
| Spine | Disc compression or misalignment | Poor core engagement in forward folds/twists |

## Yoga Cues for Safe ROM Practice

- **Warm up thoroughly** – Activate muscles before going for deep ROM.
- **Stretch with Control** – Strengthen before deepening flexibility (e.g., active hamstring engagement in Forward Fold).
- **Breathe into Expansion** – Use deep inhales to create space and exhales to deepen stretches gradually.
- **Modify & Support Joints** – Props (blocks, straps) enhance ROM safely (e.g., using a block in Trikonasana).
- **Honor Each Student's Edge** – Guide students to explore their ROM without forcing movement beyond their comfort zone.

# Chapter 3: Spine Health & Alignment Principles

The **spine** is the central axis of movement in yoga, supporting posture, flexibility, and strength. A well-aligned spine allows for **safe movement, reduces injury risk, and enhances energy flow (Prana) throughout the body**. Understanding spinal alignment and movement is crucial for both yoga practitioners and teachers.

## Structure of the Spine

The human spine has **33 vertebrae**, grouped into five regions:

| **Region** | **Vertebrae** | **Function** |
|---|---|---|
| **Cervical** | **7** - C1 to C7 | Supports head movement, neck mobility |
| **Thoracic** | **12** - T1 to T5 | Anchors rib cage, limited rotation/flexion |
| **Lumbar** | **5** - L1 to L5 | Weight-bearing, flexion/extension |
| **Sacral** | **5** (fused) - S1 to S5 | Connects spine to pelvis |
| **Coccygeal** | **4** (fused) | Tailbone, balance in seated poses |

## Natural Curves of the Spine

The spine isn't straight - it has **four** natural curves that allow it to act as a shock absorber and maintain balance. And yoga should aim to support rather than fallaten or or exaggerate these curves.

1. **Cervical Lordosis** – Inward curve at the neck
2. **Thoracic Kyphosis** – Outward curve at the upper back
3. **Lumbar Lordosis** – Inward curve at the lower back
4. **Sacral Kyphosis** – Outward curve at the tailbone

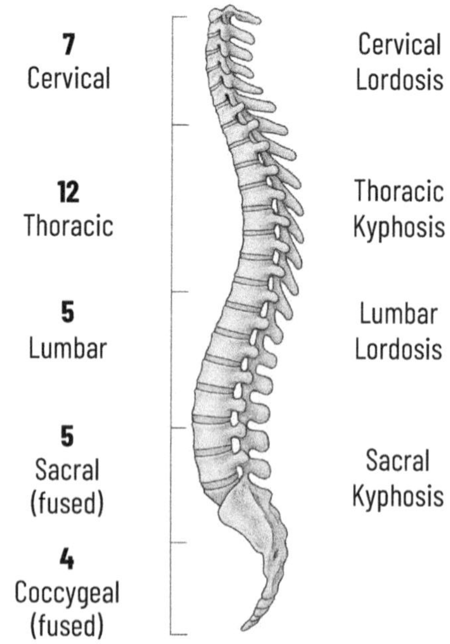

## The Five Spinal Movements in Yoga

| Movement | Definition | Pose Example |
|---|---|---|
| **Flexion** | Forward bending | Paschimottanasana (Seated Forward Fold) |
| **Extension** | Back bending | Bhujangasana (Cobra Pose) |
| **Lateral Flexion** | Side bending | Trikonasana (Triangle Pose) |
| **Rotation** | Twisting around vertical axis | Ardha Matsyendrasana (Seated Twist) |
| **Axial Elongation** | Lifting the spine upward | Tadasana (Mountain Pose) |

## Common Spinal Issues in Yoga

| Condition | Description | Prevention Tips |
|---|---|---|
| **Herniated Disc** | Bulging of disc between vertebrae | Avoid deep forward bends without core support |
| **Hyperlordosis** | Excess curve in lower back | Strengthen core, soften knees in backbends |
| **Kyphosis** | Rounded upper back, collapsed chest | Open chest, strengthen upper back |
| **Scoliosis** | Lateral curvature of the spine | Use props for symmetry, focus on alignment |

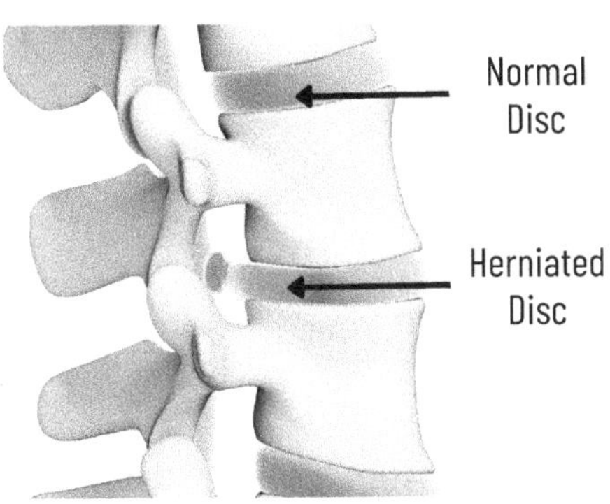

Hyperlordosis

Kyphosis

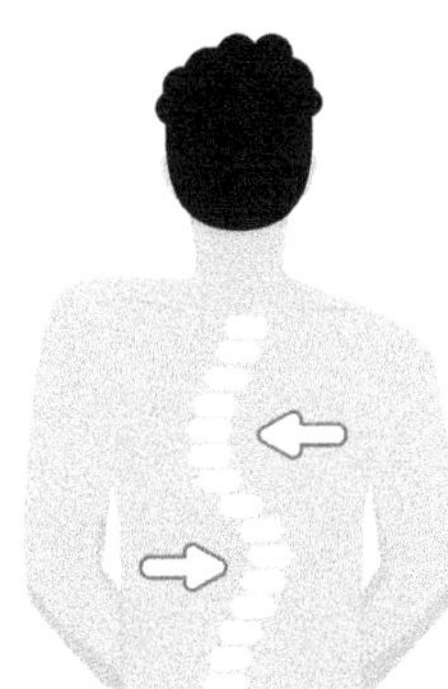
Scoliosis

# Alignment Principles for Spine Health

---

### Neutral Spine is Your Home Base

- Not tucked or arched - natural curves supported by core engagement
- Ideal in standing, seated, and balance poses

### Lift Before You Twist

- Twisting a compressed spine can cause disc damage
- **Elongate first**: *"Inhale to grow tall, exhale to rotate."*

### Protect the Cervical Spine

- In poses like Shoulderstand, use blankets to avoid neck compression
- Keep chin in line with sternum in seated postures

### Backbends Need Support

- Engage glutes + lengthen spine
- Lead with the chest, not the lower back

### Forward Bends Need Safety

- Bend from hips, not spine
- Micro-bend knees to protect lumbar discs

# Chapter 4: Muscular System & Key Muscles Used in Yoga

---

## Overview of the Muscular System

The muscular system is responsible for movement, posture, stability, and internal functions like circulation and digestion. It consists of over **600 muscles**, working together to support bodily functions and motion. The muscular system is responsible for movement, stability, posture, and joint protection in yoga practice. It consists of: Skeletal, Cardiac, and Smooth muscles.

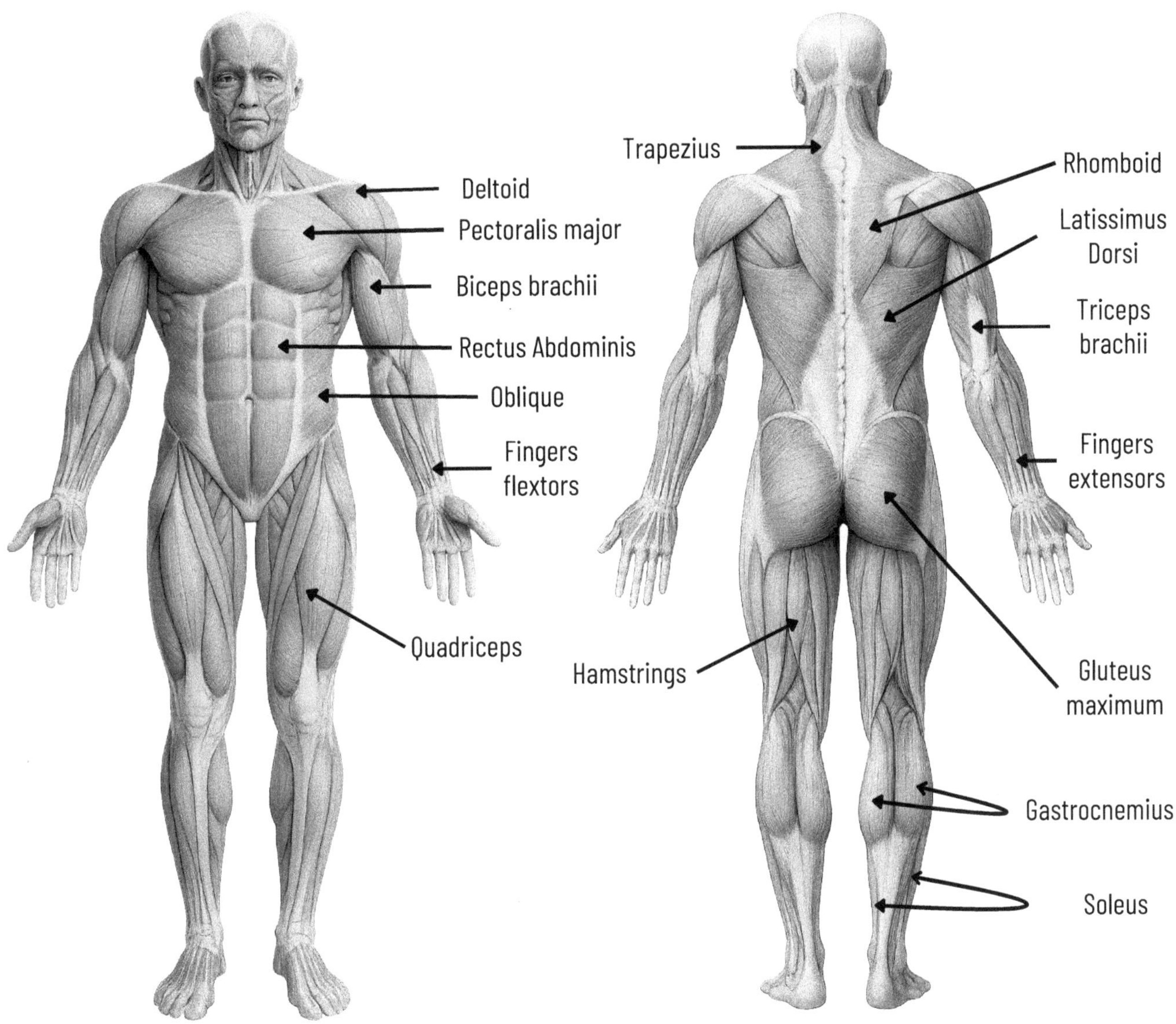


Anterior - Front View

Posterior - Back View

## Types of Muscles

There are **three main types of muscles** in the body:

Yoga primarily engages **skeletal muscles**, improving strength, flexibility, endurance, and balance.

| Muscle Type | Function | Relevance to Yoga |
|---|---|---|
| **Skeletal** | **Voluntary** muscles that move bones (attached to bones) | Primary muscles used in yoga postures (e.g., biceps, quadriceps) |
| **Cardiac** | **Involuntary**; found in the heart, responsible for pumping blood | Enhanced through breath regulation |
| **Smooth** | Involuntary; found in organs (e.g., intestines, blood vessels) | Affected by stress, digestion, breath |

## Key Muscle Groups in Yoga & Their Roles

### Core Muscles

The core provides postural support, spinal alignment, and balance in yoga poses. Muscles Involved:

**Rectus Abdominis** (front abs) – Front abdominal muscle, engaged in *Boat Pose, Plank, and Backbends.*

**Transverse Abdominis (TVA)** – Deep core stabilizer, essential for *Arm Balances & Twists.*

**Obliques (side waist)** – Support twisting poses (*Revolved Triangle, Twists*).

**Pelvic Floor** – Strengthens the lower back (*Cobra, Upward Dog*).

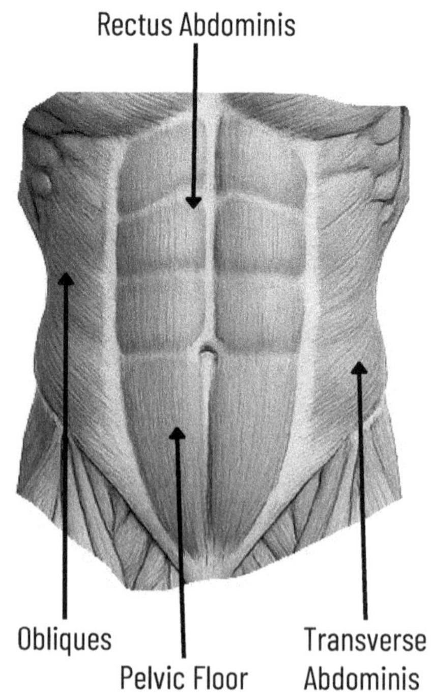

# Upper Body Muscles (Support & Strength)

The upper body muscles provide **arm strength, shoulder stability, and spinal support.**

**Muscles Involved:**

- **Deltoids (Shoulders)** – Allow arm movement & support weight-bearing poses (*Downward Dog, Handstand*).
- **Pectoral Muscles (Chest)** – Engage in chaturanga & backbends (*Upward Dog, Cobra*).
- **Triceps & Biceps (Upper Arms)** – Essential for arm balances & inversions (*Crow, Headstand*).
- **Latissimus Dorsi (Lats - Back)** – Helps in pulling & stabilizing movements (*Backbends, Twists*).
- **Trapezius & Rhomboids (Upper Back)** – Provide shoulder retraction & stability (*Shoulderstand, Plank*).

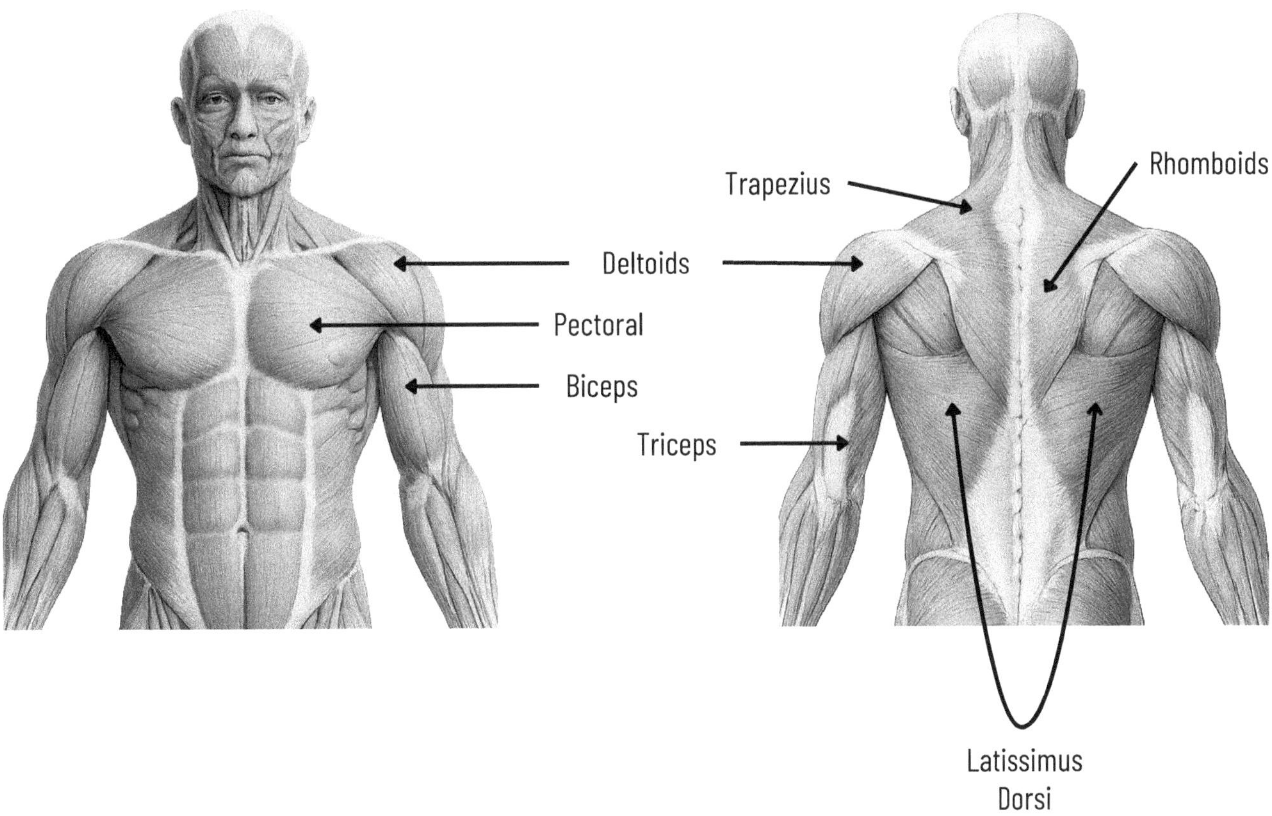

## Lower Body Muscles (Leg & Hip Muscles)

These muscles provide **grounding, balance, and flexibility** in standing and seated postures.

**Muscles Involved:**

- **Quadriceps (Front Thighs)** – Support knee extension & strength, stabilize hips *(Warrior Poses, Chair Pose)*.
- **Hamstrings (Back Thighs)** – Allow hip extension & knee flexion, important in *Forward Bends.*
- **Gluteus Muscles (Glutes)** – Help with hip stability in *Standing Balances, Backbends.*
- **Gastrocnemius & Soleus (Calf Muscles)** – Enable foot flexion, Assist balance & foot stability, Essential forwalking, running, and jumping.

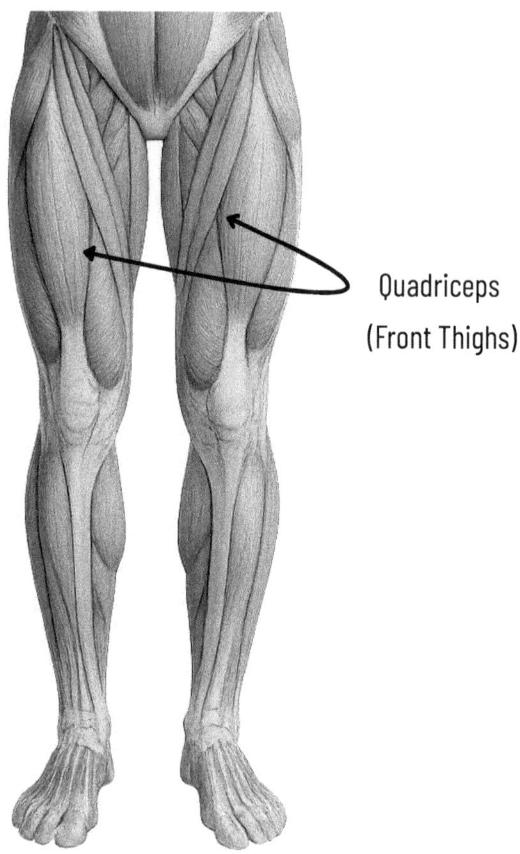


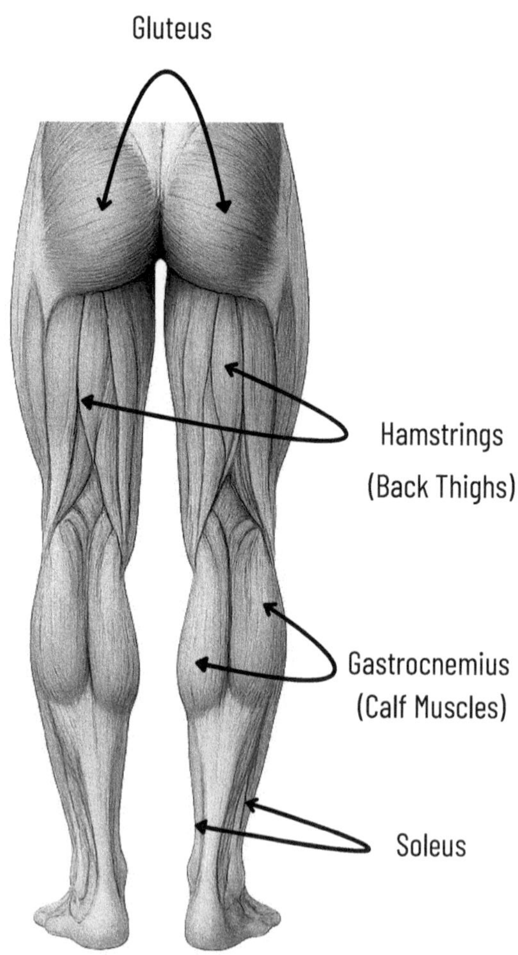

## Types of Muscle Contractions in Yoga

Muscle contractions play a key role in holding poses, transitioning between movements, and stabilizing joints. There are **three main** types of contractions:

### 1. Isometric Contraction (Holding Poses)

- Muscles generate force **without changing length**.
- **Example**: Holding Plank Pose – Core muscles stay contracted but don't move.
- **Other examples**: Warrior II, Chair Pose, Boat Pose.

### 2. Concentric Contraction (Muscle Shortening)

- The muscle **contracts and shortens**, producing movement.
- **Example**: Lifting into a Handstand – Shoulder and arm muscles contract concentrically.
- **Other examples**: Biceps engaging in Chaturanga, Hamstrings contracting in Bridge Pose.

### 3. Eccentric Contraction (Muscle Lengthening While Contracting)

- The muscle gradually **lengthens while under tension** to control movement.
- **Example**: Slowly lowering from Chaturanga – The triceps and pectorals eccentrically contract to resist gravity.
- **Other examples**: Lowering from Warrior III, Descending into a Forward Fold.

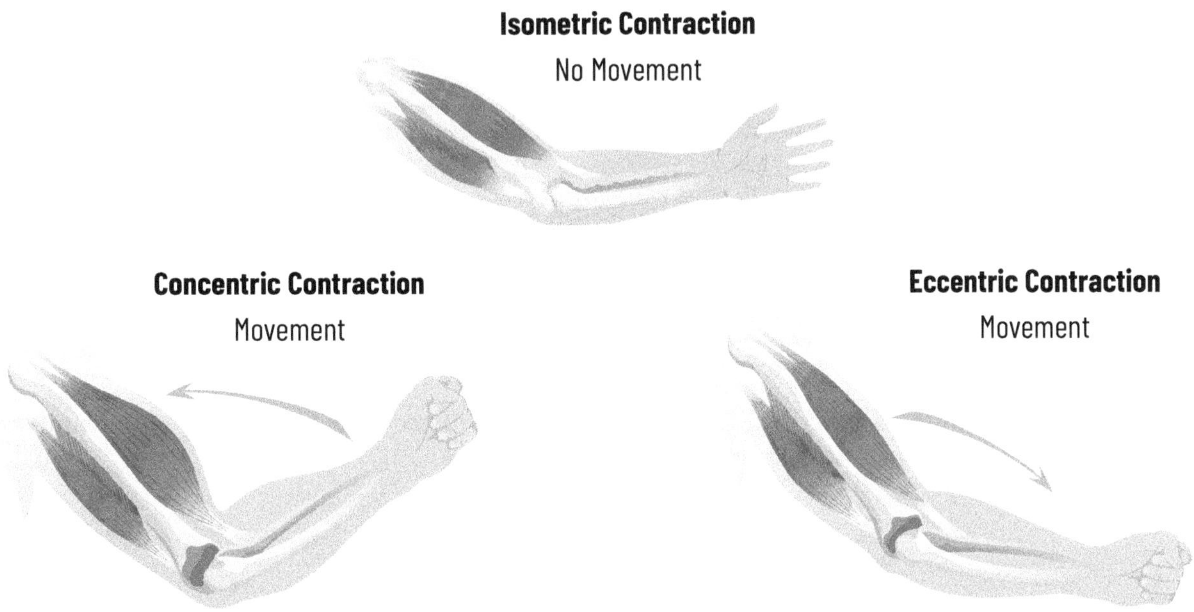

# Chapter 5: The Respiratory System & Breath Awareness

---

The respiratory system is responsible for breathing, supplying oxygen to the body, and removing carbon dioxide. It plays a vital role in **yoga**, as breath control (**pranayama**) directly affects energy levels, focus, and overall well-being.

## Functions of the Respiratory System

- **Oxygen Intake** – Delivers oxygen to the bloodstream for cellular function.
- **Carbon Dioxide Removal** – Expels waste gases produced by metabolism.
- **Regulation of pH** – Maintains the body's acid-base balance.
- **Energy & Prana Flow** – In yoga, breath is linked to **prana (life force energy)**, impacting vitality and mental clarity.

## Anatomy of the Respiratory System

The respiratory system consists of **two** parts:

### 1. Upper Respiratory Tract (Air Entry & Filtration)

- **Nose & Nasal Cavity** – Filters, warms, and humidifies air.
- **Pharynx (Throat)** – Passageway for air and food.
- **Larynx (Voice Box)** – Contains vocal cords and protects the airway.

### 2. Lower Respiratory Tract (Gas Exchange)

- **Trachea (Windpipe)** – Directs air to the lungs.
- **Bronchi & Bronchioles** – Branch into the lungs, distributing air.
- **Lungs & Alveoli** – The alveoli are tiny air sacs where **oxygen enters the blood and carbon dioxide exits.**

# Anatomy of the Respiratory System

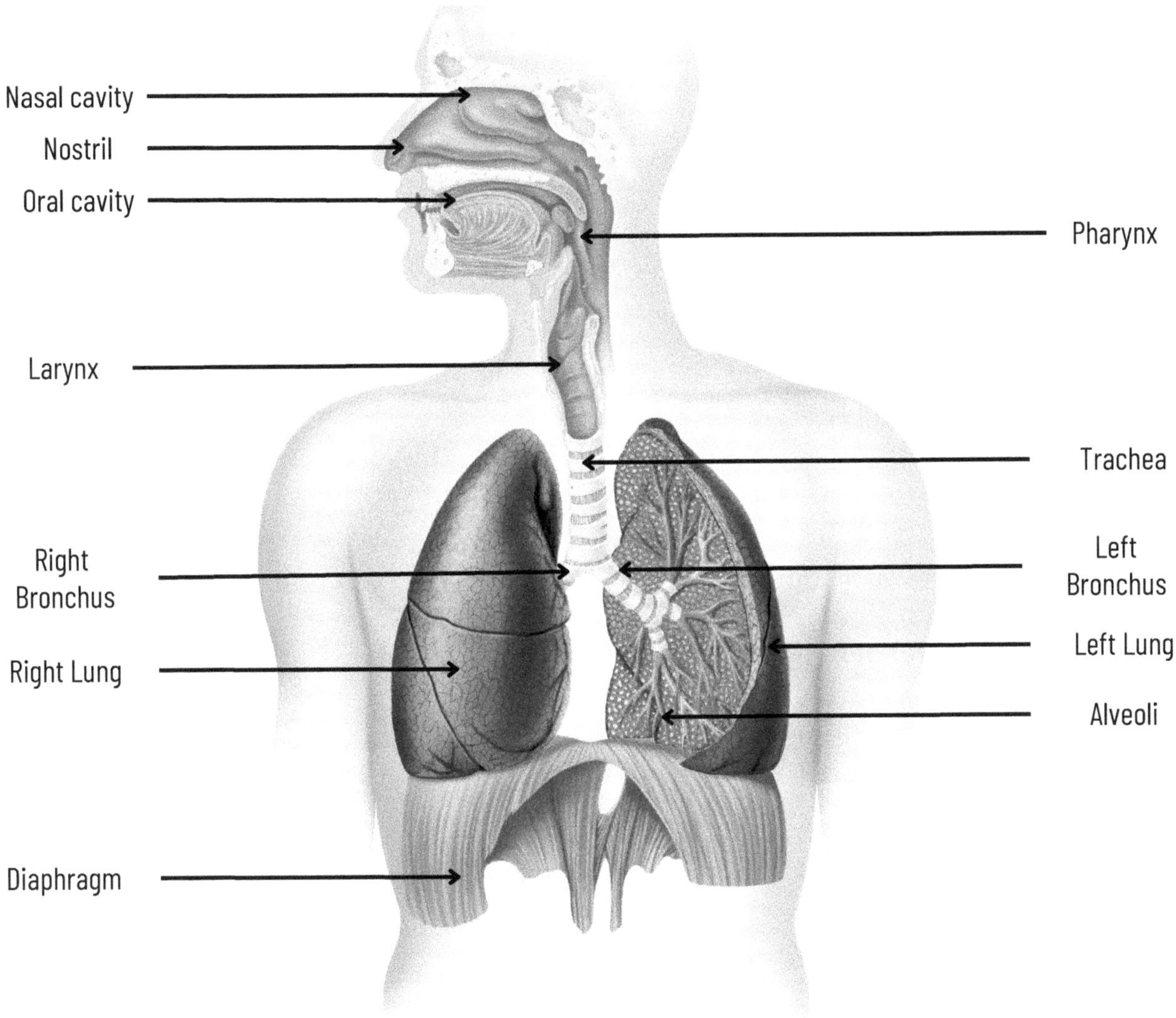

## The Breathing Process (Pulmonary Ventilation)

Breathing occurs in two phases:

### 1. Inhalation (Inspiration)

- The **diaphragm contracts** and moves downward.
- The **lungs expand**, creating a vacuum for air to enter.
- **Oxygen-rich air** fills the lungs.

### 2. Exhalation (Expiration)

- The **diaphragm relaxes**, pushing air out.
- The **lungs contract**, expelling carbon dioxide.

## The Role of the Respiratory System in Yoga

- **Pranayama (Breath Control)** – Conscious breathing techniques optimize lung capacity and energy flow.
- **Oxygenation of Muscles** – Improves endurance and flexibility in poses.
- **Nervous System Regulation** – Deep breathing activates the parasympathetic system, reducing stress.
- **Detoxification** – Exhaling releases carbon dioxide, cleansing the body.

# Chapter 6: Overview of Other Body Systems

*Digestive, Circulatory & Cardiovascular, Nervous, Endocrine System*

## Overview of the Digestive System

The digestive system is responsible for breaking down food, absorbing nutrients, and eliminating waste. In yoga, **gut health** is directly linked to **energy levels, digestion, and overall well-being**, making it essential for both practitioners and teachers to understand how digestion supports a balanced practice.

## Functions of the Digestive System

- **Ingestion** – Taking in food and liquids.
- **Digestion** – Breaking food down into nutrients (mechanical & chemical processes).
- **Absorption** – Transporting nutrients into the bloodstream for energy.
- **Elimination** – Removing waste products from the body.
- **Gut-Brain Connection** – The digestive system communicates with the brain, affecting mood and focus

## Anatomy of the Digestive System

The digestive tract is a **long muscular tube (about 30 feet long)** extending from the mouth to the anus. It consists of **two** parts:

### 1. Upper Digestive Tract

- **Mouth** – Chewing and saliva begin the breakdown of food.
- **Esophagus** – A muscular tube that moves food to the stomach via **peristalsis** (wave-like contractions).
- **Stomach** – Secretes enzymes and acids to break down food into a semi-liquid form (chyme).

### 2. Lower Digestive Tract

- **Small Intestine** – The main site for nutrient absorption into the bloodstream.
- **Large Intestine (Colon)** – Absorbs water and forms waste for elimination.
- **Rectum & Anus** – Stores and expels waste.

## Supporting Organs:

- **Liver** – Processes nutrients, detoxifies blood.
- **Gallbladder** – Stores and releases bile to help digest fats.
- **Pancreas** – Produces digestive enzymes and insulin.

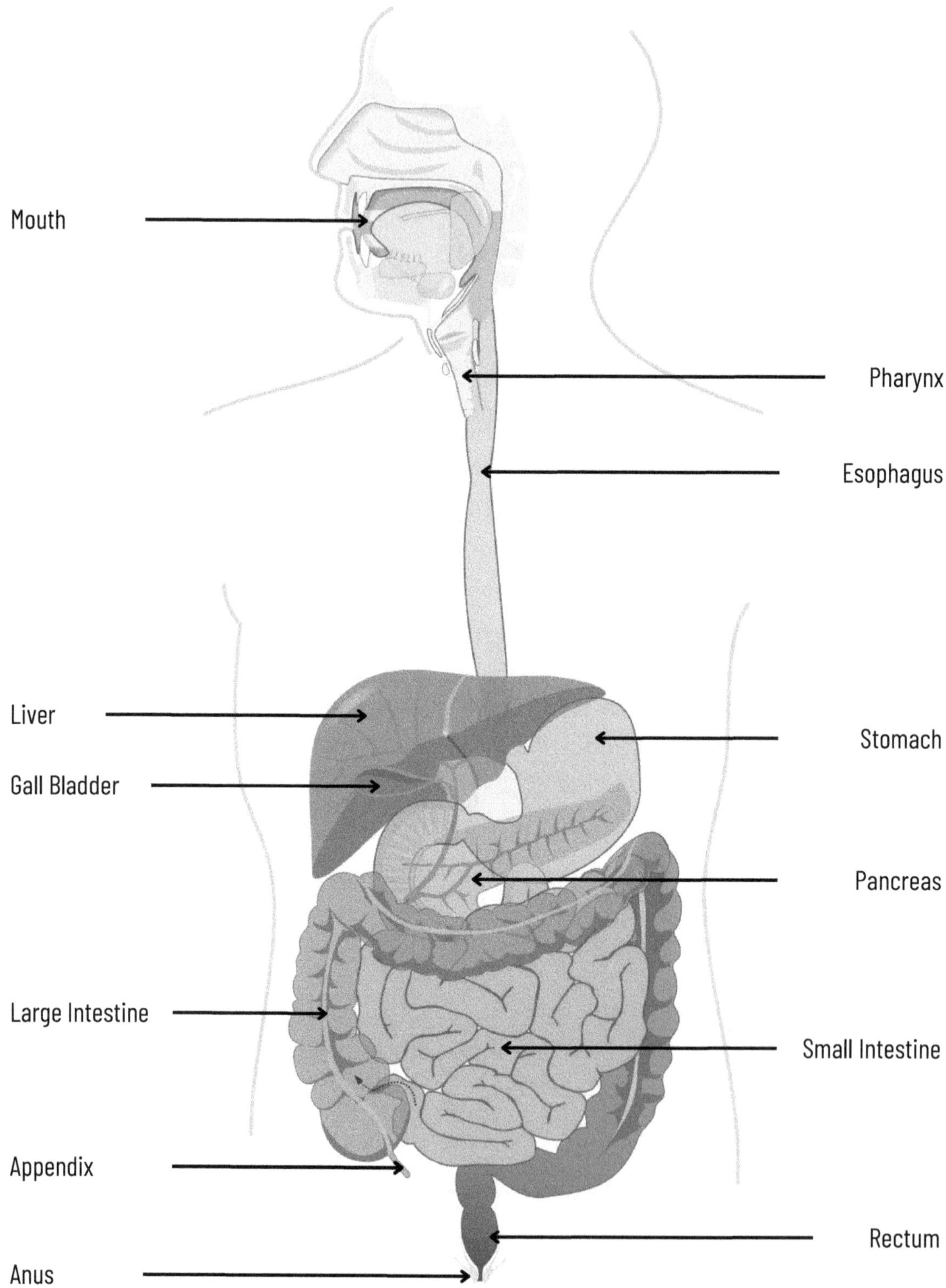

## The Digestive Process

### Step 1: Ingestion & Chewing

- **Food enters the mouth**, where chewing and saliva start breaking it down.

### Step 2: Stomach Digestion

- The stomach uses **acid & enzymes** to further break food down.

### Step 3: Nutrient Absorption in the Small Intestine

- **Enzymes** from the pancreas and bile from the liver break down fats, proteins, and carbs.
- **Nutrients enter the bloodstream**, providing energy.

### Step 4: Waste Elimination

- The large intestine absorbs water, and solid waste is expelled.

## The Role of the Digestive System in Yoga

- **Improved Digestion Through Movement** – Yoga poses **massage digestive organs** and enhance gut motility.
- **Breath Control (Pranayama) & Digestion** – Deep breathing reduces stress, aiding digestion.
- **Detoxification** – Certain poses help **stimulate the liver and intestines** (e.g., Ardha Matsyendrasana)
- **Gut Health & Energy Flow** – A well-functioning digestive system **enhances Prana (life force energy)**.

# Overview of the Circulatory & Cardiovascular System

The circulatory system, also known as the **cardiovascular system**, is responsible for transporting oxygen, nutrients, hormones, and waste products throughout the body. It plays a vital role in yoga, as efficient circulation supports energy flow (Prana), endurance, and overall vitality.

## Functions of the Circulatory System

- **Oxygen & Nutrient Delivery** – Transports oxygen from the lungs and nutrients from the digestive system to cells.
- **Waste Removal** – Carries carbon dioxide to the lungs and waste products to the kidneys.
- **Temperature Regulation** – Helps maintain body temperature by controlling blood flow.
- **Immune System Support** – Circulates white blood cells to fight infections.
- **Hormone Transport** – Delivers hormones from endocrine glands to target organs.
- **Blood Pressure Regulation** – Maintains balance between circulation and organ function.

## Anatomy of the Circulatory System

The circulatory system consists of **three** main components:

### 1. The Heart (Central Pump)

- A **muscular organ** that pumps blood through the body.
- Has **four chambers** (Right Atrium, Right Ventricle, Left Atrium, Left Ventricle).

### 2. Blood Vessels (Transportation Network)

- **Arteries** – Carry oxygen-rich blood away from the heart.
- **Veins** – Return oxygen-poor blood to the heart.
- **Capillaries** – Tiny vessels where gas and nutrient exchange occur.

### 3. Blood (The Life Force Fluid)

- Composed of **red blood cells (oxygen transport), white blood cells (immune defense), platelets (clotting), and plasma (nutrient carrier).**
- Blood regulates **body pH**, carries hormones, and supports immunity.

# Anatomy of the Circulatory System

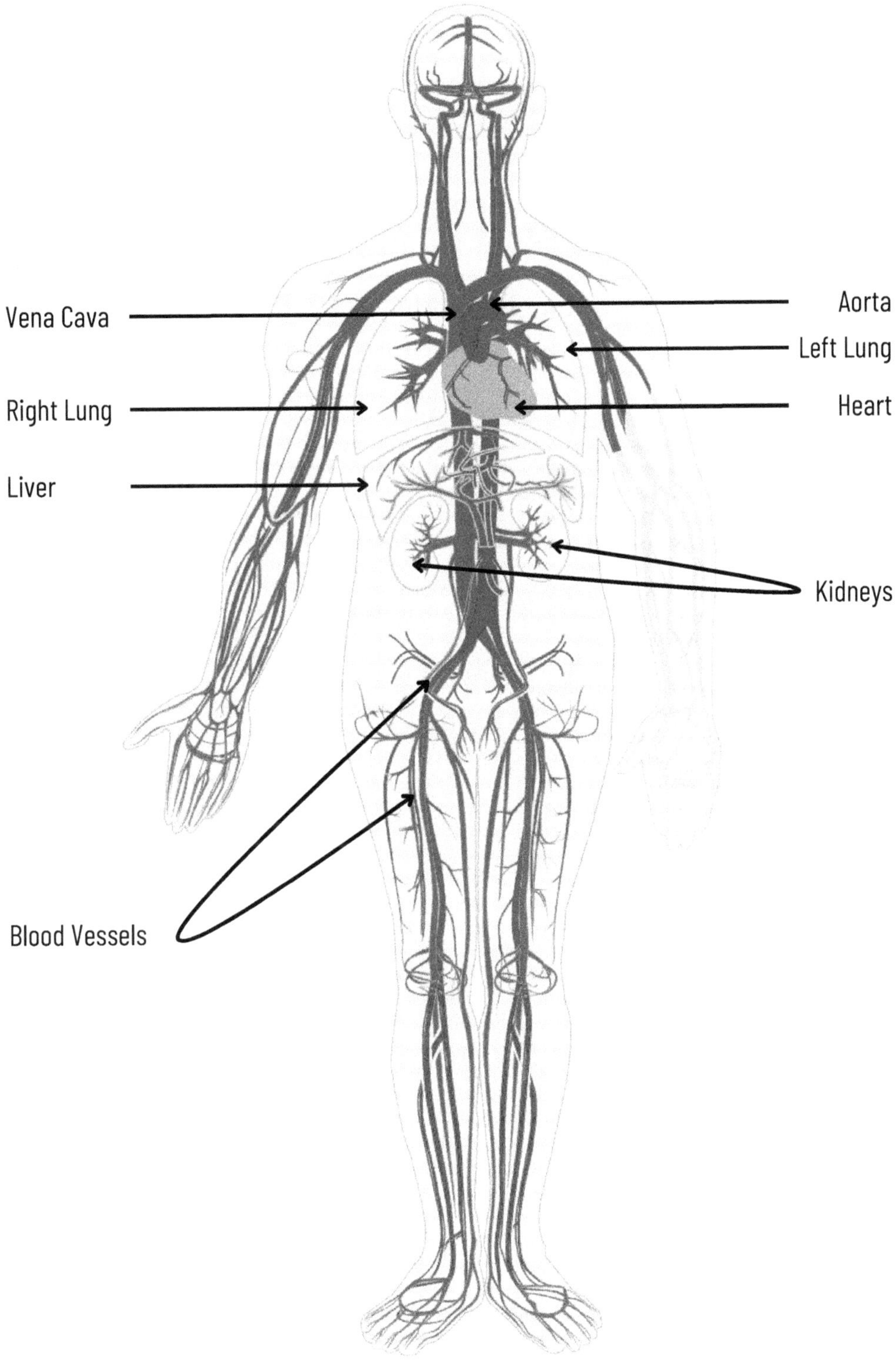

## The Circulatory Process (Blood Flow Pathway)

### Step 1: Oxygenated Blood Circulates

- The **heart pumps oxygen-rich blood** from the **lungs** through arteries to organs & muscles.

### Step 2: Oxygen & Nutrient Exchange

- Oxygen and nutrients **diffuse into tissues** through capillaries.
- Carbon dioxide and waste **enter the blood** for removal.

### Step 3: Deoxygenated Blood Returns

- Oxygen-poor blood returns to the **heart via veins**, then moves to the lungs for re-oxygenation.

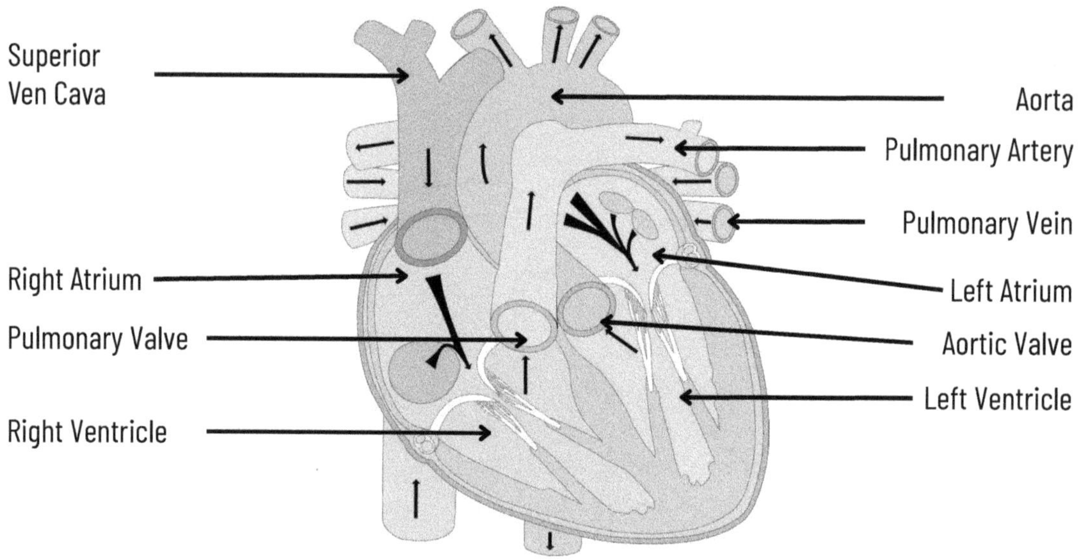


*Heart Anatomy*

## The Role of the Circulatory System in Yoga

- **Supports Energy & Stamina** – Better circulation = more oxygen for muscles, reducing fatigue.
- **Enhances Relaxation & Recovery** – Improves blood flow, reducing muscle tension.
- **Reduces Stress & Lowers Blood Pressure** – Yoga activates the **parasympathetic system,** slowing the heart rate.
- **Aids Detoxification** – Improves lymphatic drainage and waste elimination.

# Overview of the Nervous System

The nervous system is the body's command center, responsible for **sending, receiving, and processing signals** that control every function—from movement and breathing to emotions and thought processes. In yoga, understanding the nervous system helps practitioners regulate **stress, focus, and relaxation,** enhancing both physical and mental well-being.

## Functions of the Nervous System

- **Controls Movement & Coordination** – Sends signals from the brain to muscles for movement.
- **Regulates Autonomic Functions** – Manages breathing, digestion, heart rate, and reflexes.
- **Processes Sensory Information** – Interprets sights, sounds, touch, taste, and smell.
- **Manages Stress & Emotions** – Governs the fight-or-flight response and relaxation states.
- **Facilitates Learning & Memory** – Stores information and adapts through experience.

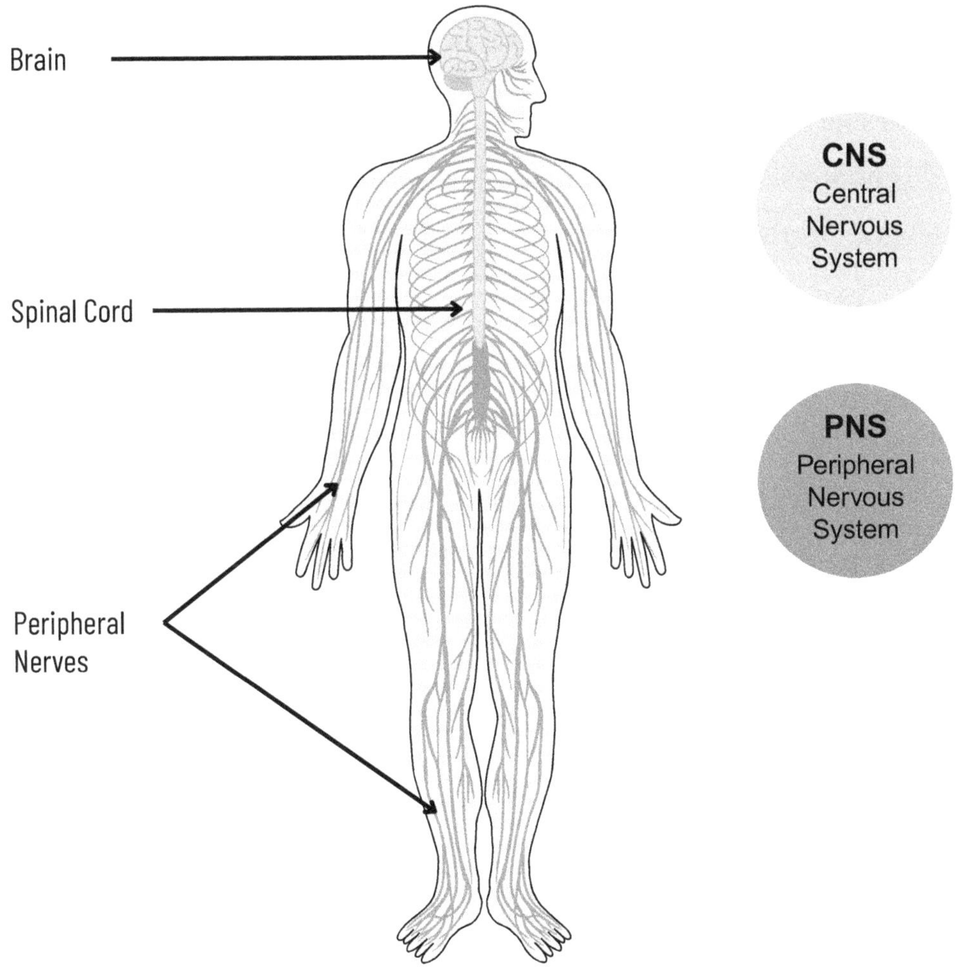


*Nervous System Anatomy*

## Anatomy of the Nervous System

The nervous system is divided into **two main parts:**

### 1. The Central Nervous System (CNS) – "The Control Center"

- Includes the **brain and spinal cord**.
- Processes and interprets information, then sends instructions to the body.

### 2. The Peripheral Nervous System (PNS) – "The Communication Network"

- Connects the CNS to the rest of the body via **nerves**.
- Includes **sensory nerves (bringing information in)** and **motor nerves (sending movement signals out).**

## The Autonomic Nervous System (ANS) – Balancing Stress & Relaxation

The **ANS** is part of the peripheral nervous system that controls involuntary functions like heartbeat, digestion, and stress responses. It has **two branches**:

#### 1. The Sympathetic Nervous System (SNS) – "Fight or Flight"

- Activated during **stress or danger** (increases heart rate, releases adrenaline).
- Prepares the body to react quickly, but prolonged activation causes tension and anxiety.

#### 2. The Parasympathetic Nervous System (PNS) – "Rest & Digest"

- Activated during **relaxation and healing** (slows heart rate, promotes digestion).
- Supports deep breathing, emotional balance, and restful sleep.

## The Role of the Nervous System in Yoga

- **Regulates Stress & Anxiety** – Yoga shifts the nervous system from **"fight or flight" to "rest and digest."**
- **Enhances Mind-Body Awareness** – Helps tune into sensations, breath, and emotions.
- **Improves Coordination & Balance** – Strengthens the brain-body connection for movement and control.
- **Supports Mental Clarity & Focus** – Meditation and breathing exercises improve cognitive function.

# Overview of the Endocrine System

The **endocrine system** is a network of **glands and hormones** that regulate essential body functions such as metabolism, growth, mood, stress response, and reproduction. Unlike the nervous system, which uses electrical signals for fast communication, the endocrine system uses **chemical messengers (hormones)** to create slow but long-lasting effects in the body.

In **yoga**, understanding the endocrine system helps in **balancing hormones, reducing stress, and enhancing overall well-being** through movement, breathwork, and meditation.

## Functions of the Endocrine System

- **Regulates Metabolism & Energy Levels** – Controls how the body converts food into energy.
- **Manages Stress Response** – Releases stress hormones like cortisol and adrenaline.
- **Supports Growth & Development** – Guides puberty, tissue repair, and aging.
- **Balances Mood & Emotions** – Affects mental well-being through hormones like serotonin and dopamine.
- **Controls Reproduction & Sexual Health** – Regulates menstrual cycles, fertility, and libido.
- **Maintains Internal Balance (Homeostasis)** – Keeps blood pressure, temperature, and hydration levels stable.

### Key Endocrine Glands & Their Role in Yoga

The endocrine system consists of several glands that produce hormones. Each plays a specific role in the body:

### Hypothalamus – "The Master Regulator"

- Located in the brain, it controls hormone release from other glands.
- Works closely with the **pituitary gland** to regulate stress, sleep, and temperature.

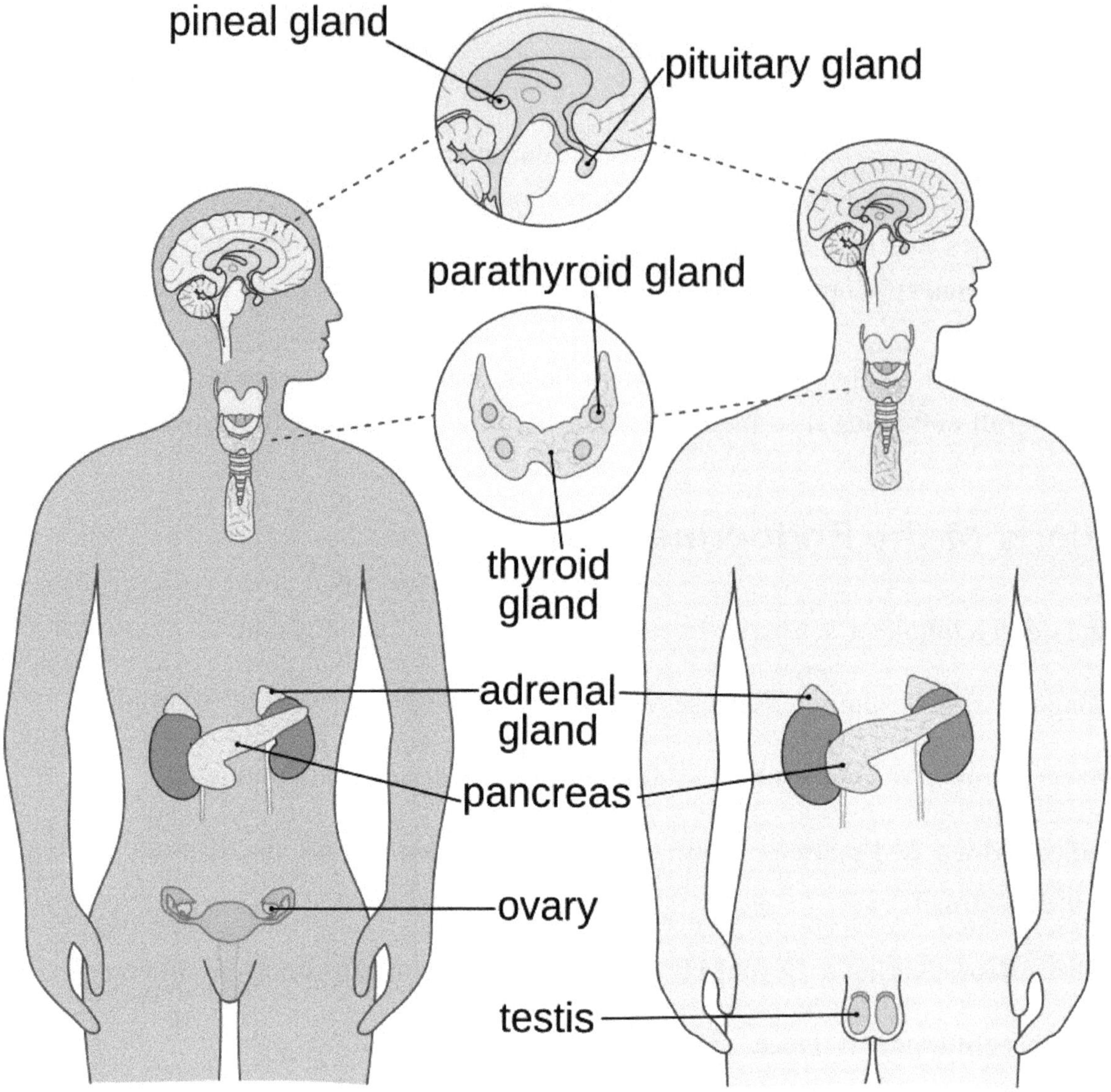


Image source: OpenStax
https://commons.wikimedia.org/w/index.php?curid=95250832

*Female* *Male*

## Pituitary Gland – "The Master Gland"

- Controls other endocrine glands and regulates **growth, metabolism, and reproduction**.
- Releases **human growth hormone (HGH)**, which supports tissue repair.

## Thyroid & Parathyroid Glands – "Metabolism & Calcium Balance"

- The **thyroid gland** controls metabolism, body temperature, and energy.
- The **parathyroid glands** regulate calcium levels for bone health.

### Adrenal Glands – "Stress & Energy Management"

- Located above the kidneys, these glands release **adrenaline and cortisol** during stress.
- Regulate **energy, blood pressure, and immune function**.

### Pancreas – "Blood Sugar & Digestion"

- Produces **insulin** and **glucagon** to regulate blood sugar levels.
- Imbalances can lead to **diabetes or energy crashes**.

### Ovaries & Testes – "Reproductive Health & Hormonal Balance"

- Ovaries (female) release **estrogen and progesterone**, regulating menstrual cycles and pregnancy.
- Testes (male) produce **testosterone**, supporting muscle strength and energy.

## How Yoga Supports the Endocrine System

- **Reduces Stress Hormones** – Yoga lowers **cortisol and adrenaline**, calming the nervous system.
- **Balances Blood Sugar** – Breathwork and movement regulate **insulin levels**, supporting metabolism.
- **Improves Thyroid Function** – Certain poses help stimulate the **thyroid and metabolism**.
- **Enhances Sleep & Mood** – Meditation boosts **melatonin and serotonin**, improving relaxation and emotional well-being.
- **Regulates Menstrual Cycles** – Gentle yoga supports **hormonal balance and reproductive health**.

# Chapter 7: Injury Prevention in Yoga Practice

Yoga is a practice of **balance, strength, and flexibility**, but improper technique, overexertion, or lack of awareness can lead to injuries. Understanding **safe alignment, mindful movement, and body limitations** is key to preventing injuries and ensuring a **sustainable yoga practice**.

## Common Causes of Yoga Injuries

- **Overstretching** – Pushing beyond the natural range of motion.
- **Improper Alignment** – Poor posture in asanas leads to joint strain.
- **Lack of Warm-Up** – Cold muscles are more prone to injury.
- **Forceful Adjustments** – Incorrect hands-on assistance can cause strain.
- **Repetitive Strain** – Overworking the same muscles without variation.
- **Holding Poses Too Long** – Can stress joints and connective tissues.
- **Ignoring Pain Signals** – Pushing through pain leads to injuries.

## Most Common Yoga Injuries

| Area Affected | Common Injuries | Causes |
|---|---|---|
| Shoulders | Rotator cuff strain, impingement | Overuse in Chaturanga, misaligned arm balances |
| Wrists | Tendonitis, carpal compression | Overloading in Downward Dog or arm balances |
| Lower back | Disc issues, muscle strain | Collapsing in forward folds or backbends |
| Knees | Ligament strain, meniscus tear | Twisting in bent-knee poses (e.g., Lotus) |
| Neck | Strain or compression | Poor alignment in headstand or shoulderstand |
| Hamstrings | Overstretching, micro-tears | Forcing into splits or deep forward folds |

### Prioritize Function Over Form

- Not every student needs to touch their toes - **encourage sensation, not shape**
- Teach **how a pose should feel**, not just how it looks

### Teach Joint Protection

- Align **knees over ankles**, **wrists under shoulders**
- Avoid hyperextending elbows, knees, or spine
- Use **micro-bends** and muscle engagement to stabilize

### Strengthen Before You Stretch

- Build **muscular support** around joints (especially shoulders and spine)
- Encourage **active range of motion**, not passive overstretching
- Don't hold deep poses for too long without engagement

### Adapt for Individual Needs

- Consider age, injuries, lifestyle, flexibility, and strength
- Offer **props**, **modifications**, and **alternative poses**
- Always ask for **injury history** in new students

### Safe Hands-On Assists

- Never force a student deeper into a pose
- Ask for **verbal or non-verbal consent** before touching
- Focus on **guiding awareness**, not "fixing" their form

### Warm-Up and Cool Down

- Never jump into deep stretches without preparing the body
- Start with **joint mobility** and **dynamic movements**
- End with **counterposes** and **restorative postures**

### Cue the Breath

- Breathing deeply prevents holding tension
- Teach exhale during effort, inhale during expansion
- Stress or anxiety from breath-holding increases injury risk

### Respect the Nervous System

- Overstretching can trigger the body's **protective response**
- Introduce deeper poses **gradually** as students develop trust
- Build **somatic awareness** through slow, mindful pacing

## Warning Signs to look out for in Class

- Holding the breath during effort
- Face grimacing or visible tension
- Sudden collapse or slumping in poses
- Twisting while joints are under load
- Forcing into flexibility without control

## The Role of Props in Injury Prevention

Using yoga props helps maintain **alignment, reduce strain, and deepen practice safely**.

- **Blocks** – Support flexibility in tight areas (under hands in Triangle Pose).
- **Straps** – Assist in stretching safely (for tight hamstrings in Forward Fold).
- **Bolsters & Cushions** – Provide support in restorative poses.
- **Blankets** – Cushion sensitive joints (under knees in seated postures)

### The Importance of Rest & Recovery

- Take breaks when needed - **restorative poses** aid recovery.
- **Hydrate & nourish** the body to support joint and muscle health.
- Prioritize **Savasana** (Final Relaxation) to integrate the practice.

# Chapter 8: Functional Anatomy in Asanas & Adjustments

Functional anatomy in yoga focuses on **how the body moves and functions in each pose**, emphasizing **alignment, engagement, and safe adjustments**. Understanding anatomy ensures that **asanas (postures) are practiced effectively** while preventing injuries and maximizing their benefits

## Applying Functional Anatomy to Asana Practice

### Mapping the Movement

Every asana involves specific anatomical actions:

- **Engagement vs. Relaxation:** Learn which muscles should contract (agonists) and which should relax (antagonists) in each posture.
- **Joint Pathways:** Understand the natural movement arcs of joints (such as the hip, knee, and shoulder) to prevent overextension or misalignment.
- **Balance of Forces:** Acknowledge the balance between gravity and muscle support; for example, engaging the core in standing poses prevents collapsing.

### Safe Entry and Exit

Proper transitions into and out of poses reduce strain:

- **Preparation:** Warm up with dynamic joint mobility before deep postures.
- **Modification:** Modify the pose if needed, like bend the knees in forward folds for tight hamstrings.
- **Easing In/Out:** Use smooth, controlled movements rather than jerky, rapid transitions.
- **Counterposes:** After a deep forward bend, offer a gentle backbend to rebalance the spine and release tension.

## Safe Adjustments & Hands-On Assists

Functional adjustments help you tailor asanas to individual needs:

**Types of Adjustments:**

- **Verbal Cues** – Guide students with clear instructions.
- **Demonstrations** – Show proper alignment.
- **Hands-On Assists** – Apply mindful pressure or support.
- **Prop Integration** - Encourage the use of blocks, straps, bolsters, etc.

## Best Practices for Hands-On Adjustments:

- Ask for permission before touching.
- Use gentle pressure, not forceful pushing.
- Work with breath, adjust during exhalation.
- Support from the base, adjust hips or shoulders first.

# Conclusion & Reflection

As yoga teachers, we are not just guiding bodies through movement—we are guiding awareness through intelligent, compassionate observation.

Understanding anatomy isn't about sounding clinical or technical in class. It's about recognizing the diversity of human form, understanding how movement works, and supporting each student's unique journey through safe, aligned, and mindful instruction.

The more you study the structure of the body, the more you'll appreciate its wisdom—and the more responsibly you can support your students' growth. Keep revisiting these concepts, not just as facts, but as tools to serve your teaching.

Remember: it's not about being perfect. It's about being present, informed, and adaptable.

## Final Reflection Prompts:

- How has learning anatomy changed how I approach my own practice?
- What cues or corrections do I now understand more deeply?
- How can I honor each student's anatomical individuality in class?

*"It is through the alignment of the body that I discovered the alignment of my mind, self, and intelligence."*

– B.K.S. Iyengar

*Wish You Health. Peace. Harmony*

In gratitude,

**Raushan Yoganta**
Founder & CEO, Yoganta

www.ingramcontent.com/pod-product-compliance
Ingram Content Group UK Ltd.
Pitfield, Milton Keynes, MK11 3LW, UK
UKHW061540190726
13845UKWH00031B/1130

9 789334 307580